CW00342169

Casta Meretrix

"The Chaste Whore"

*An Essay on the Ecclesiology
of St. Ambrose*

Giacomo Biffi
Cardinal Archbishop of Bologna

Translated by
Richard J.S. Brown (B.A. Hons)

The Saint Austin Press
296, Brockley Road, London, SE4 2RA
MM

THE SAINT AUSTIN PRESS
296, Brockley Road
London, SE4 2RA

Telephone: +44 (0)20 8692 6009
Facsimile: +44 (0)20 8469 3609

Electronic mail: books@saintaustin.org
http://www.saintaustin.org

ISBN 1 901157 34 2

Title of the original Italian edition *Casta Meretrix di Giacomo Biffi*
© Edizione Piemme Spa
Via del Carmine, 5
15033 Casale Monferrato (AL) — Italy

This edition © The Saint Austin Press, 2000.

Designed and printed by NEWTON Design & Print, London, UK
http://www.newtondp.co.uk

Casta Meretrix

We reproduce here the text of the Introduction to the proceedings of the *Studio Teologico Accademico Bolognese* for the year 1996-97. It was delivered on 30th October, 1996, and was intended to be, as it were, a prologue to the celebration of the sixteenth centenary of St. Ambrose — an initial homage on the part of the Church of Bologna to the saint recognized as one of the particular patrons of the city, and invoked as the first *defensor civitatis*.

Foreword

Casta Meretrix is one of a series of booklets by the Archbishop of Bologna, one of the more prolific and scintillating writers among the bishops of the Church, if not among all contemporary Catholic writers. He has the great gift of scholarship combined with an independent mind and a readable style.

In 1991, just before the year of European Unity, the dissolution of European borders, Cardinal Biffi issued a pamphlet entitled *Attenti all'Anticristo!* – "Beware the Antichrist!", subtitled "The Prophetic Warning of Vladimir Soloviev" – in which he warned against the worldly messianism, universal peace and prosperity of the Antichrist, portrayed by Soloviev in his *Three Conversations, and a Brief Account of the Antichrist* — a drama in which the Antichrist confronts Catholics led by Peter, the Orthodox led by John, and Protestants led by Paul. Soloviev's work, written in 1889-90, is the Russian equivalent of Robert Hugh Benson's prophetic novel *Lord of the World* (1907).

In this booklet, the Cardinal takes a look at the ecclesiology of St. Ambrose (Bishop of Milan in the years 374-397), who coined the phrase *casta meretrix*, chaste prostitute, in application to the Church. What sparked Biffi's discussion is the use of the phrase in the context of the modern and totally novel idea that the Church herself is sinful, rather than the Immaculate Bride of Christ, as we have always believed. The question of the relationship between the Church and the sins of Christians is highly relevant these days in the light of calls for the Church to "apologise" for the sins of her past, especially the sins of the past millennium. Cardinal Biffi has said openly that he is opposed to any such apologies.[1]

In the modern craze to "apologise", a few crucial distinctions are being lost. Some people have taken it upon themselves to say sorry without knowing exactly what they mean. The word *sorry* means different things depending on the context. If I say, "I am sorry your grandmother died", it is an expression of sympathy. If I say, "I am sorry for murdering your grandmother", it is an expression of contrition or repentance. If I say, "I am sorry that Brutus killed Caesar", it is an expression of regret or disagreement. When we say *sorry* for crimes of distant history, it can only be in this last sense; we are not involved enough to mean anything more.

Thus, in this sense, and in this sense alone, I can say to a man I am sorry that my ancestors made war upon his ancestors. It might even be that the effects of that injustice are still enduring: possibly, I am well situated, and his people are impoverished. Yet, at times, effective restitution becomes an impossibility. As Macaulay observes, "Is it not perfectly clear, that if antiquated claims are to be set up against recent treaties and long possession, the world can never be at peace for a day?

---

[1] See *Inside the Vatican*, May 1996.

The laws of all nations have wisely established a time of limitation, after which titles, however illegitimate in their origin, cannot be questioned."[2] Here another distinction comes into play: what St Thomas calls *culpa* and *poena*. All evil, he says, is either *culpa* (sin, crime, fault) or *poena* (penalty, punishment — and by extension, pain, harm, bad effects). The *poena* illustrates the need for compensation, restitution, atonement. Only the guilty bear the blame or *culpa*, but the *poena* can be shared. Vicarious atonement is at the heart of our religion. The All-Holy Son of God took our sins upon Himself, and made expiation for them, while remaining sinless.

Our unity in the Communion of Saints does not mean that we today are guilty of the sins of deceased members of the Church. Original Sin is transmitted by propagation, but the guilt of personal sins is not passed on to successive generations. By being baptised and entering the Church, one does not thereby inherit the guilt of past Christians, centuries after their sins! Baptism gives release from sin and all punishment. The harmful effects of some of those sins, however, may live on and need to be overcome.

While the sacrament of Confession in the Church has reached an all-time low, the new-fangled public confessions of guilt have reached an all-time high. The reason is clear: it costs nothing to apologise for sins committed by other people in the distant past. It is an easy gesture; it is the mark of false humility, the false largesse, that pretends to take responsibility where it cannot in reality — and it is a wonderful way of diverting attention from our own real sins of today. Modern

---

[2] *Frederic the Great*, Edinburgh Review, April 1842.

"apologies" about the past are a sham, because they are offered by those who were not there to those who are no longer here. A genuine apology is offered to the victims by the perpetrators. An apology offered to the dead by the innocent is merely symbolic. To be in a position to offer a real apology, one must be guilty, or responsible for those who are. In the case of sins of the distant past, no-one alive today is guilty, and no-one can claim vicarious responsibility for those who were never under his charge.

What the media have called the Pope's "apology" at the ceremony of March 12, 2000 was not really an apology in any sense of the word — neither an admission of personal or of corporate guilt, nor a defence of conduct publicly called into question. The ceremony's official title was *Universal Prayer: Confession of Sins and Asking for Forgiveness.* The word *apology* was never used. The ceremony consisted of prayers to God for forgiveness; no act of contrition was offered to victims. Rather, it was a recognition of sins committed in the past by individual Christians which have perhaps not been sufficiently acknowledged previously. But whilst we can admit there were excesses and injustices in the past (not *apologise* for them, but *admit* them), we ought at the same time uphold the validity, in some matters, of the *principles* in favour of which unwise and extreme measures were sometimes taken.

For example, we ought to reassert that heresy is destructive of social cohesion and of morality, that the Inquisition was right in trying to stop its being spread, that the person who spreads heresy amongst Catholics is committing a sin worse than murder — for while a

10

murderer or terrorist attacks people's bodies and lives, the heretic attacks people's souls and divine life. He spreads a worse infection than any earthly disease, because his infection can lead to destruction of both body and soul in Hell. The Church, commissioned by Christ to preach saving truth, must necessarily be opposed to the propagation of error. *How* she will implement her opposition to error is a matter of judgement for each age. To apply twentieth century liberal, individualist, secularist principles to churchmen of the sixteenth century Papal States, and then condemn their behaviour, is a ridiculous anachronism. It is noteworthy how the "sins" of the past meriting "apology" are only those which the modern secular world also condemns. Other crimes of the past and present are overlooked in the selection. Yet, selective apologies strike one as very insincere. In condemning the selected sins, are we really seeking belated pardon from God, or are we seeking the adulation of the world for joining it in condemning them? Are we really "apologising" for the past, or are we really making accusations at our predecessors? Are we really humbling ourselves to ask pardon from God, or self-righteously glorifying ourselves, like the Pharisee — thanking God that we are not like other men of other times, who inflicted cruel punishments and did not pay their tithes to the modern world?

One recent Beatus spoke against this modern indulgence taken at the expense of the Church: "If we love the Church, there will never arise in us a morbid interest in airing, as the faults of the Mother, the weaknesses of some of her children. The Church, the spouse of Christ, does not have to intone any *mea culpa*. But *we* do: 'mea culpa, mea culpa, mea maxima culpa'. The only true *mea culpa* is a personal one, not the one which attacks the Church, pointing out and exaggerating the human defects which, in this holy Mother, result from the presence in her of men whose actions can go far astray but which can never destroy – nor even touch – that which we call the original and constitutive holiness of the Church."[3]

The Holy Father's recent words are in this spirit, avoiding both the unreality of a pretended apology for the sins of another and the sacrilegious error of imputing guilt to the Body of Christ. Returning thus to ecclesiology, distinctions are needed if we are to answer the question: how can the Church be holy if she is formed from a race of sinners?

God has called the nations of sinners into the Church, but once they enter the Church, they are holy. *"Ex maculatis, immaculata"*, "from the sinful, the sinless one", says St Ambrose. Cardinal Biffi explains that the Bishop of Milan holds two beliefs simultaneously: the innocence of the Church, which formally, as Spouse of Christ, is never guilty of sin; and the universality of sin, which spares not even the highest-ranking churchmen. "If something is perceived in the Church which points to the infirmity of our human condition," says Pope Pius XII, "this owes nothing to her juridical constitution, but to the lamentable tendency of individuals towards evil, a tendency which her divine Founder even permits to afflict the higher members of His mystical Body, for the

---

[3] Blessed Josemaria Escriva, *In Love with the Church*, 7.

testing of the virtue of both sheep and Pastors, and for the greater merit of Christian faith in all."[4]

Sins in the Body of Christ are hers and not hers. The sins are hers, because they are of her children; they are not hers, because the mystery of her innocence is inviolable. "The Church contains sinners. But she does not contain sin. It is only in virtue of what remains pure and holy in them, that sinners belong to her," says Charles Journet in his classic work.[5] "Thus the frontier of the Church passes through each one of those who call themselves her members, enclosing within her bounds all that is pure and holy, leaving outside all that is sin and stain."[6] The Church assumes the weight of the sinner with his sins, labours for him and prays for him, and heals him of his evil, but the sin cannot be attributed to the Church herself.

Yet, we readily admit, the Church has gone through some very dark and difficult periods, laden with scandals and negligence. In times of crisis and need, God raises up saints and holy reformers to renew the face of the Church. Never in opposition to the Church, and never outside the Church, "the great reformers always burned with the Church's own flame when attempting to renew it."[7] They "found a remedy for the Church's evil in the Church itself, for it is only in the holiness which it possesses that there can be found a remedy for the sin which afflicts it."[8]

---

[4] *Mystici Corporis*, 1943, Part I.
[5] *The Church of the Word Incarnate*, Sheed and Ward, London 1955, p. xxvii.
[6] Ibid.
[7] Bishop L.Z. Legaspi, O.P., *The Church We Love*, University of Santo Tomas, Manila 1982, p. 174; 1997 ed., p. 191.
[8] Ibid.

13

May God raise up these much-needed Saints today, "lest the heathens say: 'where is their God?' But our God is in the heavens. He does whatever He wills." (Ps. 113/115.) He is the Lord of time and history, and the fate of the Church and the world is in His hands. When the time has come, He will come to judge the living and the dead.

Fr Peter Joseph

Vianney College

Wagga Wagga
Australia

I.
St. Ambrose's use of the phrase "Casta Meretrix"

The Fate of the Term in Modern Times

"Casta Meretrix", a "chaste whore", is a somewhat surprising oxymoron, especially since it is usually used in reference to the Church.

In recent times, following its use by von Balthazar (in *Sponsa Verbi*, Brescia, 1985), the phrase has enjoyed a moderately good fortune. Indeed, every so often it is brought to my attention, whenever, in fact, I rashly declare my conviction that the Church *as such* cannot be called "sinful" — for it is always thrown at me by people who seem satisfied that they have clinched the argument: "But the Church," they retort, "is a *'casta meretrix'*, according to the Church Fathers!" They place so great an emphasis upon the noun in this phrase that the accompanying adjective is almost completely ignored.

"According to the Church Fathers", they say: yet it has never been considered a particularly worthy thing for Christians to speak ill of the Church (which no ancient profession of the Faith ever failed to call "Holy"). Rather, this has always been the habit of those "others", i.e. the non-believers. Is it legitimate, then, for the faithful to add their voices to this chorus of slanderers, even in order to encourage an "open and constructive dialogue"?

The more timid among them would never find the courage to do so, if they were not able to throw in this very phrase, "according to the Church Fathers".

"According to the Church Fathers"

To hear them say this, one would almost think that there were a universal consensus on this point; that not a single one of those great Doctors of the Faith of the early centuries would have failed to assign this picturesque title to the Church; that the name "casta meretrix" would be an irrefutable element of all traditional theology[9].

"According to the Church Fathers..." Bolstered by such an authoritative testimony, the Catholic heart is reassured, and can talk with an easy conscience of the "sins of the Church".

And yet how many of these Fathers of the Church actually used this term? And who exactly are they?

A better judgement notwithstanding, only one of them does: St. Ambrose. No one else spoke of the "casta

---

[9] Let us cite, for example, H. Küng, who, in the following passage, whilst clearly convinced of his assertion, takes little care to substantiate his claim: "There is only one Church, which is at one and the same time holy and sinful, a 'casta meretrix', just as it has often been called since patristic times..." (H. Küng, *La Chiesa*, Brescia, 1969, p. 379).

meretrix" before him, and not one of the Fathers after him chose to imitate his usage[10].

Rahab, Type of the Church

Ambrose did, in fact, use the expression in question once and once only, in his meditation on Rahab, the woman of Jericho who is mentioned in the book of Joshua.

Ambrose says that she "as a *type* was a prostitute, but as a *mystery* is the Church, united now to the Gentiles by the sharing of the sacraments":

> "…Typo meretrix mysterio ecclesia, sacramentorum consortio populis copulata gentilibus…" (*In Lucam* VIII:40).

The "typical" use of Rahab – a contradictory character, to whom was attributed both an unworthy profession and a praiseworthy and providential action – was already a classic in Christian literature.

Matthew's Gospel had recalled her in the genealogy of Jesus (Matthew 1:5). The Letter to the Hebrews had featured her as an example of the faith which saves (Hebrews 11:31). St. James, concerned with other aspects of theology, had emphasised her justification obtained through works, i.e. through the good deed that she did for the Hebrew scouts (James 2:25). Clement of Rome,

---

[10] We know this to be a guaranteed fact for the Latin Fathers since it is confirmed by computer wordsearch techniques. As for the Greek Fathers, we can only say that no similar expression used in reference to the Church has been drawn to our attention from their writings.

almost as though trying to synthesise and reconcile the two texts, had written, "Through her faith and her hospitality, Rahab the prostitute was saved" (*I ad Corinthios* 12:1).

After Clement, who dwells a long time on the episode of Joshua 2:1–21, reading it in the light of the Redemption worked by Christ (cf. *I ad Corinthios* 12:1–8), a definite ecclesiological interpretation of the figure of Rahab is clearly delineated — from Justin to Irenaeus, to Origen, to Cyprian. Indeed, it is through reflection upon the "house of the prostitute" – the only house in Jericho which preserved its occupants from death – that the famous principle emerged of *extra Ecclesiam nulla salus*:

"No one could be deceived in this regard", writes Origen, "no one could be mistaken: outside of this house, that is to say outside of the Church, there is no salvation" (*Om. in Iosue* 3:4).

Cyprian in turn writes, "Do you think that you can live if you detach yourself from the Church, building yourself other houses and different dwelling places, when Rahab, prototype of the Church, was told that anyone who left the door of her house would be guilty?" (*De unitate ecclesiae* 8)[11].

---

[11] In Cyprian the principle of "extra Ecclesiam nulla salus" is linked to the truth of the maternity of the Church: "no one can have God for a father who does not have the Church for a mother" (*De unitate ecclesiae* 6).

What is meant by "casta meretrix"?

Ambrose presumably had Origen's commentary in mind above all else as he reflected upon this point. However, his own thinking developed in a very individual way:

"Rahab – who as a *type* was a prostitute, but as a *mystery* is the Church – showed in her blood the future sign of Universal Salvation amid the world's carnage; she does not refuse to unite herself with numerous fugitives, and is all the more chaste in the extent to which she is closely joined to the greater number of them; she is the immaculate virgin, without a wrinkle, uncontaminated in her modesty, plebeian in her love, a chaste whore, a barren widow, a fecund virgin".

> "In suo sanguine inter excidia mundi publicae futurum salutis insigne Rahab illa, typo meretrix mysterio ecclesia, indicavit, quae multorum convenarum copulam non recusat et quo coniunctior pluribus eo castior, immaculata virgo, sine ruga, pudore integra, amore plebeia, casta meretrix, vidua sterilis, virgo fecunda" (*In Lucam* III:23).

This passage deserves to be commented upon in detail:

Typo meretrix mysterio ecclesia – This means to say that the activity of prostitution belongs to the "figure", not to the reality figured. We cannot therefore make hasty transpositions from "type" to "antitype"; first we have to clarify in what sense and from what point of view the comparison has been established.

Multorum convenarum copulam non recusat – The clarification of the previous point is given immediately: the Church can be recognised in the woman of Jericho *only* because she does not refuse to unite herself to the multitude of the "fugitives", i.e. those who, disorientated and scattered throughout the earthly city, seek in her a shelter from perdition.

Quo coniunctior pluribus eo castior – There is, however, a fundamental difference. The obligingness with which the Church opens her doors to all, in the same way as those women of easy virtue, not only requires no blameworthy action, but is even a sign of her faithfulness to her mission (and hence to her Bridegroom who has assigned this mission to her).

Immaculata virgo, sine ruga, pudore integra – Almost so as to prevent any misunderstanding which could arise from such an undeniably daring comparison, here Ambrose evokes – and even surpasses – the impassioned language of St. Paul in Ephesians 5:27 (where Paul exalts the "ecclesiam non habentem maculam aut rugam aut aliquid huiusmodi").

It is worth noting that Ambrose's text is not concerned with the *eschatological* condition into which the Lord wishes to carry His Bride. "Immaculata virgo, sine ruga, pudore integra" is, for the Bishop of Milan, exactly the same Church who, on her course through history, welcomes and offers salvation to men who are "scattered" ("convenae").

Amore plebeia – The expression is a little daring, but so intensely rich in meaning that it is almost untranslatable. "Plebeius" in the Latin writers is a word that always has at least a whiff of scorn about it. That it could be adopted by a highly cultured Roman patrician in order to qualify the Bride of Christ, is sufficient evidence of the truly revolutionary innovations introduced by Christianity into Roman society.

The Church is "plebeia" in her love; that is to say that there is nothing aristocratic and exclusive in her attentions, which are directed towards all without distinction. Rather, if she has any preferences, these tend to be for the simple, the humble and the poor. Ambrose, as we know, had a certain degree of hostility towards positions of privilege, so much so in fact that he wrote, "Let no one presume, because he is rich, that greater homage is due to him. In the Church a person is rich if he is rich in faith."

> "Nemo praesumat quia dives plus sibi deferendum. Ille est dives in ecclesia qui fide dives est" (*Ep. extra coll.* 14:86).

Three Images

Ambrose's meditation in this passage on the nature of the Church employs three images, which we must consider simultaneously if we wish fully to understand the mystery of the Church. The Church is at once whore, widow and virgin: "meretrix casta, vidua sterilis, virgo fecunda". We are immediately offered a clear explanation of these three titles.

The Church is a "chaste whore, since many lovers frequent her because of the attractions of love; yet she is free from the contamination of sin".

The Church is a "barren widow, because in the absence of her husband she has not known child-bearing (but then her husband arrived, and thus she has brought forth this nation and this people)".

The Church is a "fecund virgin, because she has given birth to this multitude, as the fruit of her love; not, however, through the intervention of concupiscence".

> "Casta meretrix, quia a pluribus amatoribus frequentatur cum dilectionis illecebra et sine conluvione delicti...; vidua sterilis, quae viro parere non norit absente (venit vir et hunc populum plebemque generavit); virgo fecunda, quae hanc genuit multitudinem cum fructu amoris, sine usu libidinis" (*In Lucam* III:23).

In Conclusion

If we consider the original meaning of the expression "casta meretrix", then far from being a reference to sinfulness and guilt, this phrase actually refers to the *holiness* of the Church; and this reference is made not merely by means of the adjective, "casta", but through the noun "meretrix" as well. Furthermore, this holiness consists as much in her clear and unswerving loyalty to Christ her Bridegroom ("casta") as in her desire to bring everyone together so as to lead them to Salvation ("meretrix").

In addition to this, the expression does not belong "to the Fathers", but to Ambrose alone, who coined this phrase in the unprejudiced freedom of his faith, with the sole intention of exalting the Bride of Christ.

II.
The Beauty of the Bride

A Synthesis

The passage on Rahab which we have just examined is clearly motivated by affection and admiration for the Bride of Christ, a feature which is characteristic of the entire literary output of St. Ambrose. If the phrase "casta meretrix" is, as we have seen, a *hapax*, then throughout Ambrosian theology the joyful perception of the beauty of the Church is constantly taken for granted.

This is particularly evident in the last ten years of his work, when his "discovery" of the Canticle of Canticles offered a more suggestive form of language to the basic intuitions which he already possessed.

We find in the *Apologia David altera*, "Christ desired the beauty of His Church, and prepared to unite Himself to her in matrimony":

> "Ecclesiae suae Christus speciem concupivit
> et paravit eam sibi in uxorem adsciscere"
> (*Apologia David altera* 48).

Indeed, it is by means of the Church that the King's own beauty is reflected onto us, and in this way becomes perceptible to us (for it is usually hidden to our pilgrim eyes):

> "Decor et gloria vultus eius ecclesia" (*In ps. 48*, 11).

The value and charm of the Church (like that of the consecrated virgin, who is, in a sense, her "icon") does not subsist in her loquacity, but in the depth of her sentiments and in the hidden reality of the mysteries that she celebrates:

> "Virginitatis dos quaedam est verecundia, quae commendatur silentio. Ideo et ecclesiae gloria intus est, non utique in multiloquio, sed in sensibus vel in penetralibus sacramentorum" (*De institutione virginis* 5).

In the last letter of the saintly bishop, the Canticle is glossed in the following way:

" 'You are a walled garden, O sister my bride, a walled garden, a sealed fountain'. Christ says these words to the Church, and wants her to be a virgin without stain, without a wrinkle ... And no one can doubt that the Church is a virgin".

> " 'Hortus – inquit – clusus, soror mea sponsa, hortus clusus, fons signatus". Christus hoc dicit ad ecclesiam quam vult esse virginem sine macula, sine ruga... Nec

potest dubitare quisquam quod ecclesia virgo sit" (*Ep. extra coll.* 14:36–37).

The two reasons for the Church's beauty

From this simple affirmation we can proceed to a more substantial examination, asking ourselves where the Church's beauty (or her holiness, which is the same thing) originates.

If we reflect well upon this, the answer is already implicitly contained in the title "casta meretrix", and in the context in which this title is found. The principal reason for the beauty of the Church is her relationship with Christ; the subordinate reason is because of her mission to save the men whom Christ has entrusted to her.

Protected by the Charm of Christ

The Church knows herself to be the target of demoniacal attacks, which attempt to take her virtue by storm. Yet the Church also knows that she has in Christ an invincible ally and a comforting defence:

> "Dicit ecclesia: "Ego civitas munita, ego civitas obsessa": munita per Christum, obsessa per diabolum. Sed non debet obsidionem vereri cui Christus adiutor est" (*Exameron* VI:49).

The Church also knows that she is subject to a thousand temptations and tricks; but she also knows that her Saviour exercises a more decisive charm over her, which keeps her safe from hallucinations and trickery:

"Many put the Church to the test, yet no incantation from the magic arts can ever harm her. The enchanters have no power in that place where the canticle of Christ resounds daily. She has her enchanter: the Lord Jesus, by means of Whom she has been able to render ineffective the incantations of the enchanters and the venom of the serpents…"

> "Multi temptant ecclesiam, sed sagae artis ei carmina nocere non possunt. Nihil incantatores valent ubi Christi canticum cotidie decantatur. Habet incantatorem suum dominum Iesum, per quem magorum incantantium carmina et serpentum venena vacuavit" (*Exameron* IV:33).

The Bridegroom

Why is the Church so sure that she is protected by Christ from all pitfalls and weaknesses? For the simple reason that He is her Bridegroom.

We can understand nothing of the "value" of the Church, if we are deprived of the enlightenment that such nuptial imagery affords us. In its proper sense it reveals the existence of a connection between the People of God and their Redeemer, an intimacy, a communion rooted in their very *being*. This connection is so important that one cannot even begin to consider the *reality* of the Church as something autonomous and separate from the Only-Begotten Son of the Father.

He is her only bridegroom (*De patriarchis* 22: "Ipse est solus vir ecclesiae"), and He has no rivals.

The Church is the Church in proportion to, and by virtue of, her status as the Bride. If anyone dares to introduce a division into this relationship, even mentally or hypothetically, by failing to recognise her centrality in God's design and her absolute uniqueness, then he departs from the Truth, and anything he may say about the Church becomes unreal and, in a sense, fictitious:

"Only the Father could have arranged this marriage … The bridegroom is Christ, the bride is the Church, a bride by her love, a virgin by her intact purity … God has joined them together, let the Jew divide them not. All are adulterers who desire to adulterate the Truth of Faith and Wisdom".

> "Ille solus has nuptias potuit copulare… Vir Christus, uxor ecclesia est, caritate uxor integritate virgo… Deus coniunxit, Iudaeus non separet. Adulteri sunt omnes qui adulterare cupiunt fidei et sapientiae veritatem" (*In Lucam* VIII:9).

For this reason it is the Church alone, and not the Synagogue, who is able from this moment onwards to pour forth authentic acts of love towards the Lord:

"The Church does not cease to kiss the feet of Christ, and for this reason in the Canticle of Canticles she requests not one but many kisses, since – just like the Holy Virgin Mary – she is attentive to all of His teachings, she accepts His every word... and keeps all His sayings in her heart. Therefore only the Church can kiss Him, in her capacity as His Bride; indeed the Kiss is the sign of a wedding and the token of a marriage. For this reason, what sort of kisses can the Jew give, who does not believe in the Bridegroom; what sort of kisses can he give, if he does not yet know that the Bridegroom has come?"

> "Ecclesia non cessat osculari pedes Christi et ideo non unum sed multa oscula in Canticis canticorum exigit, quae velut sancta Maria ad omnes eius est intenta sermones, omnia eius verba excipit... et omnia eius dicta conservat in corde suo. Sola ergo ecclesia habet oscula quasi sponsa, osculum enim pignus est nuptiarum et praerogativa coniugii. Unde Iudaeo oscula qui non credit in sponsum, unde Iudaeo oscula qui adhuc sponsum venisse non novit?" (*Ep. extra coll.* 1:18).

Jesus, Origin of the Church

This nuptial imagery does, however, have its limits and its inconveniences: it places the husband and wife on a level of equality with one another, and implies that both partners have an existence prior to their relationship. Yet this is not the case with Christ and the Church, and Ambrose is well aware of it.

The comparison can, however, be made adequate if it is considered in the light of the first man and the first woman: Eve is genuinely Adam's wife and binds herself to him in such a way as to constitute "one flesh" (cf. Genesis 2:24); but before this she was drawn in her entirety *from* him, and he, before becoming her husband, was her "origin":

"The last Adam is Christ, the rib of Christ is the life of the Church ... She is Eve, the mother of all the living".

> "Novissimus Adam Christus est, costa Christi vita ecclesiae est" (*In Lucam* II:86).

In any case, the Lord Jesus is at the origin of everything (cf. *In ps. 43*, 39: "Semen omnium Christus"); indeed He is the beginning and the end of the universe:

"He is the first and the last; the first, because He is the Creator of all things; the last, not because He has an end, but because He is the Fulfilment of all things without exception":

> "Ipse est primus et novissimus (cf. *Ap* 1:17): primus, quia auctor est omnium; novissimus, non quod finem inveniat, sed quod universa concludat" (*De Sacramentis* V:1).

However, since in Ambrose the order of Creation and the order of Redemption are never separated, this affirmation of Christ's "supremacy" becomes all the more pertinent when it is applied to the Church:

"Where Faith is, there we have our beginning and our end; where there is disbelief, there is neither a beginning nor an end. The Church, which has Christ, has an origin: Christ is indeed the origin of the Church... She also has an end, because He is the first and the last... However the Synagogue has neither a beginning nor an end, because it neither found the road to follow at the beginning, nor at the end the reason for hope".

> "Ubi fides est, et initium et finem habemus; ubi perfidia, nec initium nec finis est. Ecclesia principium habet, quae Christum habet; Christus enim ecclesiae principium est... Habet et finem, quia ipse est primus et novissimus... Synagoga nec initium nec finem habet, quia nec in principio invenit quod sequatur, nec in fine quod speret" (*In ps. 118*, 20:3)[12].

One Body

The imagery of the "bride" leads naturally into that of the "body", in line with the ecclesiological interpretation by St. Paul of the statement in Genesis about "one flesh" (see Ephesians 5:22–32).

The Church constitutes, together with her Saviour (her "head"), a single living organism.

---

[12] On the theme of "Christ the Origin of the Church", see G. Toscani, *Teologia della Chiesa in sant'Ambrogio*, Milan, 1974, pp. 299–313.

By virtue of this identification, attacks upon the Church and upon individual believers can be considered without hesitation to be attacks upon the Son of God:

"Christ was not attacked once only. Of course, he was attacked once in the body that He assumed inside the Virgin; but he has been attacked more times in that body which is the Church. For we are the body and the members of Christ".

> "Non semel appetitur Christus. Appetitus est semel in suo corpore quod suscepit in virgine, appetitus est frequenter in eo corpore quod est ecclesia. Nos enim sumus corpus Christi et membra" (*In ps. 118*, 16).

The Privileges of the Church

It is from her status as the "bride" and the "body" of Christ – which is the origin of all her beauty, and which establishes her in an objective condition of holiness – that she derives the privileges which exalt her in the eyes of the angels.

We can even say that the existence of the Church is the cause of the Redeemer's glory, His "crown", the cause of the Universe's joy:

> "Quae est corona gloriae nisi ecclesiae, quae caput suum Christum coronat? Quae iucunditas universae terrae nisi domus populi christiani, aula sanctorum…?" *(In ps. 118*, 15:11).

Ambrose's enthusiasm brings a multiplication of images, as he tries to do justice to the great preciousness of God's Church, which contains every cause of joy:

"It is pleasurable to contemplate ... this people which is the instrument for the harmony of God's work, among whom the music of God's word resounds, among whom the Divine Spirit performs His work. It is pleasurable to contemplate this temple which is the sanctuary of the Trinity, the abode of sanctity, the holy Church within which shine all the celestial ornaments...".

> "Spectare voluptati est... populum hunc divinae operationis organum, in quo divini modulamen resultet oraculi et Dei Spiritus intus operetur; templum istud, sacrarium Trinitatis, sanctitatis domicilium, ecclesiam sanctam in quae refulgent aulaea celestia..."
> (*Exameron* III:5).

Sacrarium Trinitatis – The Church, by virtue of her conjugal status and her bond of love, is the masterpiece of the Trinity and the sanctuary which houses the epiphany of the Three Divine Persons. It is worth our while reading, in this regard, the following exhortation addressed by Ambrose to the newly baptised:

"The Church is beautiful. It is for this reason that the Word of God says to her: "You are wholly beautiful, my beloved, and there is nothing in you worthy of reproach", because the Fault has been overwhelmed... For this reason the Lord Jesus – drawn by the desire for so great a love, by the beauty of her clothing and by her gracefulness, (since now there is no taint of guilt in those who have been purified) says to the Church: "Place me as the seal upon your heart, as the seal upon your arm", that is to say: you are fair, my beloved, you are wholly beautiful, lacking in nothing! "Place me as a seal upon your heart", because through this your faith shines brightly in the fullness of the sacrament. Even your works shine and reveal the image of God, in the image of Whom you were made... Remember that you have received the seal of the spirit, "the Spirit of wisdom and of understanding, the Spirit of counsel and of strength, the Spirit of knowledge and of piety, the Spirit of the fear of God", and that you must preserve what you have received. God the Father marked you out, Christ the Lord confirmed you and placed the Spirit in your heart as a pledge, as you have learned from the writings of the Apostle [cf. 2 Corinthians 1:21–22]".

> "Formosa est ecclesia. Unde ad eam verbum Dei dicit: "Tota formosa es, proxima mea, et reprehensio non est in te", quia culpa demersa est... Unde dominus Iesus et ipse invitatus tantae studio caritatis, pulchritudine decoris et gratiae, quod nulla iam in ablutis delicta sorderent, dicit ad ecclesiam: "Pone me ut signaculum in cor tuum, ut sigillum in brachium tuum", hoc est: Decora es, proxima mea, tota formosa es, nihil tibi deest. "Pone me ut signaculum in cor tuum", quo fides tua pleno fulgeat sacramento. Opera quoque tua luceant et imaginem Dei praeferant, ad cuius imaginem facta es... Unde repete, quia accepisti signaculum spiritale, "spiritum

sapientiae et intellectus, spiritum consilii atque virtutis, spiritum cognitionis atque pietatis, spiritum sancti timoris", et serva quod accepisti. Signavit te Deus Pater, confirmavit te Christus dominus, et dedit pignus in cordibus tuis, sicut apostolica lectione didicisti" (*De mysteriis* 39:41–43).

The Source of Sanctification

It is necessary for anyone who is persuaded, under the guidance of the Word of God, that all salvation and all sanctification issue into the world from the Church, to believe in her beauty and her sanctity. This is not to say, of course, that the action of redemption and renewal does not fully belong to Christ; nonetheless it does pass by way of the Bride who is joined to Him, and who supports Him in this task. She is not, however, a support in a purely instrumental and almost mechanical fashion, but is like someone who puts his heart and mind into an activity; and does so to such an extent that we can even attribute to her the salvific functions of the Lord Jesus. For example, that of the "Door":

"Since the Door is Christ, who cries, "Whoever passes through me shall be saved", so also can the Church be called the Door, because she opens up to the people the way to Salvation".

> "Quia ianua Christus est, qui ait: "Per me si quis introierit salvabitur", et ecclesia ianua

nuncupatur, quia per ipsam patet populis aditus ad salutem" (*In ps. 118*, 22:38).

The parable of the woman kneading dough (Luke 13:20) is redirected by Ambrose towards the probing of that mystery of the Church which allows Jesus, Wisdom of the Father, to penetrate deep into our inmost being:

"May Holy Church, who is prefigured typologically in this woman of the Gospel, and of whom we are the flour, hide the Lord Jesus in the most secret recesses of our souls, until the brilliance of celestial wisdom is blended into the inmost sanctuary of our being".

> "Sancta ecclesia, quae typo mulieris istius evangelicae figurantur, cuius farina nos sumus, dominum Iesum in interioribus nostrae mentis abscondat, donec animi nostri secreta penetralia color sapientiae caelestis obducat" (*In Lucam* VII:187).

The imagery is now much denser, but the intention remains of conveying to us the fact that Christ's richness and His divine vitality are given expression and brought within our reach precisely through the arcane reality of the Church:

"The Church is the wine-press of the eternal fount, because the fruit of the celestial vine overflows into her".

> "Ecclesia torcular est fontis aeterni, in qua caelestis vitis fructus exundat" (*De Spiritu Sancto* I:1).

For this reason she, who is founded upon Peter, contains nothing that is death-bringing:

"Where Peter is, there is the Church; and where the Church is, there is not death but eternal life".

> "Ubi Petrus ibi ecclesia; ubi ecclesia ibi nulla mors sed vita aeterna" (*In ps. 40*, 30).

The Mother

It is apparent from what has already been said that the Church enjoys a condition of fertility. By virtue of her spousal relationship, which embellishes her with the Word of God, and steeps her in the Holy Spirit, the Church begets the new members of Christ:

"To Him was the Church wedded, and she – filled with His Word and with the Spirit of God – has given birth to the body of Christ, that is, to the Christian people".

> "Cui nupsit ecclesia quae, verbi semine et spiritu Dei plena, Christi corpus effudit, populum scilicet christianum" (*In Lucam* III:38).

Through her immanence in Christ, she becomes the principle of life, in direct opposition to Eve, the origin and figure of sinful humanity, for thus even she can obtain salvation:

" 'That which was made in Him was life' – as Ambrose reads John 1:3-4. If you ask what this 'life' is, if you are troubled by what was done in Him, then here is your answer: this life is without doubt the Church! She was created in Him, from His rib; in Him Eve was resuscitated. And yet Eve is life (i.e. that which was made), since Eve, who was lost, was saved by means of the Church".

> " 'Quod factum est in ipso vita est" ... Si quaeris quae vita sit, [si] moveat quod factum est in ipso, accipe: nempe vita ecclesia est. In ipso facta est, in eius costa, in ipso resuscitata Eva. Eva autem vita est, hoc est: quod factum est, quia Eva quae perierat salva facta est per ecclesiam" (*In ps. 36*, 37).

Fecund because Immaculate

Ambrose clearly has a conviction, right from the start of his pastoral ministry, that every capacity that the Church has for conferring holiness – and hence every power that the Church has in her capacity *as* Church – derives entirely from her perfect loyalty to Christ, the origin of every redeeming action.

Ambrose gained this conviction through reflection upon the allegory of the Wedding: in the light of this imagery he gathered immediately the necessary connection that there is in the mystery of the Church between virginal conjugality and fertility.

The Church is supernaturally active and effective by virtue of belonging entirely to the Lord Jesus; as much as she is a mother, so also is she a virgin bride, unswerving in her fidelity.

In his first work, *De virginibus* (presumably composed only three years after his ordination as bishop) he demonstrates this conviction, a conviction which will remain with him right the way into his last works:

"Holy Church is immaculate in her marital union: fecund through her childbearing, she is a virgin because of her chastity, and a mother to her children. We therefore are born of a virgin, who has conceived not through man but through the Spirit. We are born of a virgin not amidst physical pains but amidst the rejoicing of angels. She feeds us as a virgin, not with the milk of her body but with the milk spoken of by the Apostle, when he says that he has suckled the adolescent people of God in its age of weakness. What married woman has more sons than Holy Church? She is a virgin through the holiness that she receives in the sacraments and is the mother of nations. Even Scripture bears witness to her fertility, saying: 'The sons of the abandoned woman are more numerous than those of the woman who has a husband.' Our mother knows no man, but yet has a spouse – for in the same way as the Church is to the nations, and the soul is to individuals, she is married to the word of God as to her eternal spouse without any slight against her modesty, empty of any offence, but fecund in spirit".

> "Sancta Ecclesia immaculata coitu: fecunda partu, virgo est castitate, mater est prole. Parturit itaque nos virgo non viro plena, sed spiritu. Parit nos virgo non cum dolore membrorum, sed cum gaudiis angelorum.

Nutrit nos virgo non corporis lacte, sed apostoli, quo infirmam adhuc crescentis populi lactavit aetatem. Quae igitur nupta plures liberos habet quam sancta Ecclesia, quae virgo est sacramentis, mater est populis, cuius fecunditatem etiam scriptura testatus dicens: "Quoniam plures filii desertae magis quam eius quae habet virum"? Nostra virum non habet, sed habet sponsum, eo quod sive Ecclesia in populis sive anima in singulis Dei verbo sine ullo flexu pudoris quasi sponso innubit aeterno effeta iniuriae, feta rationis" (*De virginibus* I:31).

The Church's Relativity

Nowadays our ears are perhaps not used to such an exaltation of the Church – of her beauty, her holiness. However Ambrose does not believe that, in celebrating the Bride of Christ, we could ever commit the sin of exaggeration; and there is surely truth in what he says.

The danger, if there is one, lies elsewhere: it is that of making the Church into an absolute, as though there were something in her, worthy of praise and appreciation, which did not derive from her relationship with Christ, and which was not a simple reflection of that unique and incomparable value of the Son of God made man.

Yet Ambrose does not run such a risk: the conviction that "Christ is all" is so strongly rooted in him, that he is not even touched by a suspicion that something positive could derive from others, except as a mere reflection of the original richness of Him in Whom all things were created, and all things were reconciled (cf. Colossians 1:16–20).

As regards our subject, his comparison of the Church with the moon is of fundamental importance; the symbolism inspires him in two ways.

The first of these concerns the "lunar" nature of the Church, who, in the course of her history, passes through periods of fortune and periods of misfortune, in an alternation of different "phases", yet without her substance ever being compromised.

The second – which has an even greater theological importance – is an appreciation and a reaffirmation of the perfect dependence of every value and glory of the Church upon the "Sun of Justice", to whom is attributed everything that is true, good and beautiful about the Church:

"The Church, like the moon, often wanes and then waxes anew. As an effect of these wanings she comes to deserve to increase and grow in size, despite the fact that under the persecutions she became smaller and was crowned by the martyrdom of her confessors. She is the true moon, who derives the light of immortality and of grace from the perennial light of her brother; for the Church does not shine with her own light, but with that of Christ, and she takes her own splendour from the Sun of Justice... Truly you are blessed, O moon, since you have deserved such importance! For this reason I venture to call you blessed; not on account of your new moons, but because you are the symbol of the Church: in the former you are a slave; in the latter you are an object of love".

> "Ecclesia sicut luna defectus habet et ortus frequentes, sed defectibus suis crevit et his meruit ampliari, dum persecutionibus minuitur et confessorum martyriis coronatur. Haec est vera luna, quae de fraterni sui luce perpetua sibi lumen immortalitatis et gratiae mutuatur. Fulget enim ecclesia non suo, sed Christi lumine et splendorem sibi arcessit de sole iustitiae… Beata plane, quae tantum insigne meruisti! Unde te non tuis numeniis, sed typo ecclesiae beatam dixerim; in illis enim servis, in hoc diligeris" (*Exameron* IV:32).

Summary

As we have seen, the conceptual content of the phrase "casta meretrix" is developed to the full in all of Ambrose's meditations on the Church. The Church is a mystery of holiness mainly because she is "casta" (i.e. perfectly faithful to the Lord Jesus who has united her to Himself), but also because she is called to give herself to all people through her sanctifying actions.

If we force the syntax a little, we could even say that "casta" indicates her status as the Bride of Christ, and "meretrix" her status as the mother of all men.

If we venture beyond purely sciolistic analyses, however, there does exist the problem of understanding how the transcendent and uncontaminated reality of the Church actually relates to the evil which contaminates all worldly affairs, and in which even the Bride of Christ today finds herself immersed. It is certain that Ambrose would have been well aware of this, for he was not an abstract idealist who shied away from the affairs of men. Indeed, few pastors have ever had the scale of involvement in the contemporary vicissitudes of Church, State and society that he had.

It follows, then, that we must test him further upon this question, and pursue our exposition of his thought along these lines.

III.
The Church and the Presence of Evil

Three Questions

By virtue of her nature as the "bride" and the "body" of the Son of God, the Church (in her most profound level of being) cannot receive into herself anything which is contaminated, and by function of her specific mission to impart holiness, can only be "full of grace". However, given that she lives within time and walks along the dusty and snare-ridden roads of the world, she necessarily has to have something to do with iniquity, that contaminant universally present in the world since the beginning of human history.

Let us therefore seek to understand what Ambrose's thinking was on this subject, basing our investigation around three questions:

What influence upon the Church does that "external" evil have, i.e. the demonic forces which are actively hostile to the plan of God?

In what measure does sin, which certainly exists within the Christian community, extend into the "mystery" of the Church, i.e. her true nature?

What theological significance can be assigned to the apparent barrenness and moral weakness with which the Church presents herself to the eyes of the world?

The Church and "External" Evil

A straightforward answer to the first question can be found immediately: it is normal for the Church to be the butt of hostility and misunderstanding. We must consider once again the guarantee of her authenticity:

"In tribulations the Church finds her foundations; she is established in storms and tempests, in cares and sorrows…".

> "In tribulationibus fundatur ecclesia; in tempestatibus et in procellis, in sollicitudinibus et maerore… praeparatur" (*In ps. 48*, 4).

The torments which she encounters can only help to purify her and to test her, as happens with gold:

"Like fine gold, the Church is not damaged by fire; indeed she is made more splendid, until that day when Christ shall come into His Kingdom to recline His head upon the faith of the Church".

> "Sicut aurum bonum, ita ecclesia cum uritur detrimenta non sentit, sed magis fulgor eius augetur, donec Christus veniat in regnum suum et reclinet caput suum in ecclesiae fide" (*In ps. 118*, 3:7).

Ambrose often has recourse to nautical imagery:

"The Church", he says, "is a ship which, with its sail of the Lord's cross filled with the wind of the Holy Spirit, sails happily through this world".

> "Navis ecclesia est, quae pleno dominicae crucis velo sancto Spiritu flatu in hoc bene navigat mundo" (*De virginitate* 119).

Being a ship, she cannot avoid the furies and storms of the sea:

"The Church is struck by the waves of worldly cares, but is not overwhelmed by them; she is buffeted, but not weakened; she easily contains and calms the jolting of the waves and the assaults of bodily passions. She observes the shipwreck of others, whilst she herself is immune to them and escapes danger; she is always ready to be lit up by Christ, and, illuminated in this way, to acquire joy".

> "Ecclesia tunditur saecularium curarum fluctibus, sed non subruitur; caeditur, sed non labefactatur; commotiones fluctuum et insurrectiones passionum corporalium facilis premere ac mitigare. Spectat aliorum naufragia, ipsa immunis et exsors periculi, parata semper ut inlucescat sibi Christus atque eius inluminatione iocunditatem adquirat sibi" (*De Abraham* II:11).

Since she places this invincibility at the service of men, she can also be compared to a safe harbour, where all may find refuge:

"She lives in the middle of the waves, but is not shaken by them, and is ready to give help, rather being exposed to danger herself. Thus, if people who are pressed by violent storms wish to take refuge in this harbour, the Church offers herself to them as an harbour of salvation, and calls into her lap of tranquillity with open arms anyone who lives in danger, showing them a secure mooring".

> "Circa fluctus habitat, non fluctibus commovetur magisque ad subveniendum parata quam periculo obnoxia, ut si qui tempestatibus acti gravibus confugere ad portum velint, praesto sit ecclesia tamquam portus salutis, quae expansis bracchiis in gremium tranquillitatis suae vocet periclitantes locum fidae stationis ostendens" (*De patriarchis* 27).

Called as she is to struggle against the forces of evil, she uses weapons which have nothing in common with those of her enemies:

"The Church does not conquer the powers that oppose her with the weapons of the world, but with spiritual weapons which have the strength of God and are capable of destroying the powerful ramparts of the spirits of evil... The weapon of the Church is faith; the weapon of the Church is prayer which conquers the enemy".

> "Ecclesia non armis saecularibus vincit adversarias potestates, sed armis spiritalibus, quae sunt fortia Deo ad destruendas

munitiones et altitudinem nequitiae spiritalis … Arma ecclesiae fides, arma ecclesiae oratio est, quae adversarium vincit" (*De viduis* 49).

The Church and the Synagogue

Before we move our attention onto such transgressions as exist within the life of the Church, we must confront the delicate subject of the relationship between the Church and Ancient Israel. Ambrose has an understanding of this subject which differs from the one predominant today, and it is precisely because of this that we can find it useful to compare our own ideas with those found in his teachings.

There exists for him a sort of twofold link between the Synagogue and the Church: with a contrasting comparison on the one hand, and one of continuity on the other.

The contrasting comparison is based upon the idea that the "Israel of the flesh" has gone astray, and her riches have all passed to the "Israel of God" (to use the words of St. Paul):

"Truth also existed in the Old Testament and used to belong to the Jewish people… Yet since successive generations of Jews went astray from the conduct of their forefathers, Truth was withdrawn from them and passed over to the Church".

> "Est veritas et in veteri testamento, quae fuit ante in populo Iudaeorum... Sed quia posterior suboles Iudaeorum a patribus moribus deviavit, recessit ab illis veritas et ad ecclesiam venit" (*In ps. 118* 12:19).

Today, only the Bride of the Lord possesses the fullness of the Revelation and the Law of God (cf. *In ps. 118* 22:33).

Only the Bride of Christ is able, through her faithful love, to bring back springtime to the earth:

"The Synagogue loved once, the Church loves now and does not change her affections for Christ... To the Church is said, "The winter has passed, it has gone away: the flowers have appeared on the earth, the time of the harvest has arrived". Before the coming of Christ, it was winter; since His coming, behold the flowers of the spring, the harvest of the summer".

> "Synagoga dilexit, ecclesia diligit nec unquam circa Christum suum mutat adfectum... Ecclesiae dicitur: "Hiems abiit, discessit sibi: flores visi sunt in terra, tempus messis advenit". Ante adventum Christi hiems erat, post adventum Christi flores sunt veris et messis aestatis" (*Exameron* IV:22).

The Continuity of the "Israel of God"

Even more important is the perspective through which Ancient Israel is seen as the first stage of existence of the "Israel of God". According to this way of looking at things, the life of the Church begins with the calling of Abraham: in this way the entire history of salvation has but one subject, who, following various betrayals and recoveries, finally achieves that condition of unalterable fidelity which is suited to the New Covenant.

From this point of view, we can talk of a Church which passes not only from laws to graces, but even from guilt to a regained innocence. In this way, the category of sin can be admitted and employed even by those who reflect upon the true reality of the Church, which, as we have seen, is intrinsically holy.

Abraham is therefore the father of all those who believe in Christ; the story of the Church begins with the promise which was made to him:

" 'In you shall be blessed all the tribes of the earth". Note that it was to him, first of all, that the unification of all peoples and the assembling of the Most Holy Church was promised by the divine oracle. It is for this that he has rightly been designated *progenitor*, since he, first of all, merited the solemn promise of the Institution of the Church".

> " 'Benedicentur in te omnes tribus terrae'. Vides ergo congregationes gentium et sacrosanctae ecclesiae coetum oraculo divino huic primo esse promissum. Et ideo is auctor generis debuit designari, qui

instaurandae ecclesiae sponsionem primus emeruit" (*In Lucam* III:7).

Be that as it may, we cannot go backwards. Whosoever passes from the Synagogue to the Church goes in the natural direction of salvation history; but whosoever passes instead from Church to Synagogue puts his own salvation in jeopardy, because he departs from the design of God:

> "Nemo de ecclesia ad synagogam sine periculo transit salutis" (*In Lucam* VI:52).

In the light of these considerations we can understand what would be meant by attributing to the Church a preceding condition of guilt; it would mean alluding to her existence as the people of the Old Covenant.

"Holy Church... says in the Canticle of Canticles, 'I am the black and beautiful daughter of Israel': black through guilt, beautiful through grace; black through her natural condition, beautiful through her redemption".

> "Ait in Canticis canticorum: 'Nigra sum et decora filia Israel'': nigra per culpam, decora per gratiam; nigra per condicionem, decora per redemptionem" (*De Spiritu Sancto* II:112).

The Church and Sinful Humanity

It must be said straightaway that sometimes Ambrose considers even the "Gentiles" (i.e. humanity as such, leaving aside Revelation) as the first phase of the journey which brought the human family to the Church. Yet even here (and with a greater freedom of expression), we can talk of sins, from which the Church was later freed by the mercy of God; and she was freed by becoming the Bride of Christ:

"Christ alone is the Bridegroom, to whom is united in marriage that Bride who comes from all peoples, who before was poor and needy, but is now rich with the harvest of Christ".

> "Solus Christus est sponsus, cui illa veniens
> ex gentibus sponsa ante inops atque ieiuna,
> sed iam Christi messe dives innubat…" (*De
> fide* III:72).

"Since the Church was formed through the unification of the Gentiles (i.e. from sinners) how is she able to turn out *immaculate* from such a mixing together of contaminated peoples, unless she was first of all purified from sin by the Grace of God, and following this preserved from blame through a state of life exempt from sin? For this reason she is not immaculate from her origins – an impossible thing for human nature – but she does appear immaculate, by the grace of God and by her own state of life, because she sins no more".

> "Cum ecclesia ex gentibus, hoc est ex
> peccatoribus congregata sit, quomodo ex
> maculatis immaculata potest esse, nisi primo
> per Dei gratiam, quod abluta a delicto sit,
> deinde quod per qualitatem non peccandi
> abstineat a delictis? Ita nec ab initio

immaculata – humanae enim hoc impossibile naturae – et per Dei gratiam et qualitatem sui, quia iam non peccat, fiat ut immaculata videatur" (*In Lucam* I:17).

We can then speak of a state of guiltiness of the Church *only* if we begin her history with men not yet redeemed (*necessarily* "contaminated"). However, when considering the family of the baptised as such, the title best suited is that of "holy", and sin cannot be considered a fact of the Church.

"Ex maculatis immaculata"

There appears on the above-mentioned page the formula "ex maculatis immaculata", which I am in the habit of quoting offhand so as to express the *constitution* of the Bride of Christ. In reality, however, as we have seen, Ambrose uses this formula rather to indicate a succession of two different conditions: those of before and after baptism.

Nonetheless, this does not seem to be so grave an abuse (leaving to one side the correctness of my quotation), if we recognise that, within the scope of the "Church-Guilt" relationship, the Bishop of Milan's viewpoint is a result of the simultaneous presence within his mind of the following two convictions:

The blamelessness of the Church; who, in her formal role as the Bride of Christ, is never made the target of negative moral judgements;

The universality of sin; which does not even spare the men who have the highest responsibilities within the Church. This fact is vividly illustrated by the sense that Ambrose has of his own sinfulness, as in his famous reflection upon Tamar, the daughter-in-law of Judah, and her rather dubious initiatives:

" 'Tamar is more just than I''. It might indeed happen that a young girl could fall into sin, deceived and overcome by circumstances, which act as an incitement to sin. We old men sin also; the law of our flesh rebels within us against the law of our mind and drags us as prisoners towards Sin, so that we do things we do not want to do. That young girl has an excuse in her age, whereas I have none: indeed, she is still learning, whereas we should be instructing. Therefore, 'Tamar is more just than I''. Do we accuse someone else of being greedy? Then let us try to remember if we ourselves behave in a greedy way; and if we do … then let us each say of ourselves, 'Tamar is more just than I' ''.

> " 'Iustificata magis Thamar quam ego''. Fortasse adulescentula lapsa sit occasionibus, quia delictorum fomites sunt, decepta et praecipitata. Peccamus seniores, repugnat in nobis lex huius carnis legi mentis nostrae et captivos nos in peccatum trahit, ut faciamus quod nolumus. Illi de aetate suppetit excusatio, mihi iam nulla: illa enim debet discere, nos docere. Ergo 'iustificata est magis Thamar quam ego''. Incusamus alicuius avaritiam? Recordemur, si ipsi nihil avare facimus, et si fecimus…

dicamus   singuli: 'Iustificata   est   magis
Thamar quam ego' " (*De paenitentia* II:74).

The Church and the sins of Christians

The Church, who remains "holy" within herself, cannot however be said to be a stranger to the world of sin: she views it from a position of proximity and comes into contact with it in her daily life, so much so that she can feel within herself, like a discomfort or a wound, every blameworthy action of her members.

She asks to be healed from these wounds like the woman with the haemorrhage in the Gospel:

"Your family does not say, 'I am well, I have no need of a doctor", but says, 'Heal me, Lord, and I shall be healed; save me and I shall be saved". For this reason the figure of Your Church is to be found in that woman who drew near to You from behind and touched the fringe of Your garment, 'saying to herself, "If I succeed in touching his garment, I shall be saved" '. This Church, then, confesses her wounds; this Church wants to be healed".

> "Non dicit familia tua: Sana sum, medicum non quaero, sed dicit: 'Sana me, domine, et sanabor, salva me et salvabor". Denique ecclesiae tuae species est in illa, quae accessit retro et tetigit fimbriam vestimenti tui, 'dicens intra se, quia si tetigero vestimentum eius, salva ero". Haec ergo ecclesia confitetur vulnera sua, haec curari cupit" (*De paenitentia* I:31).

Wounds of this sort are both hers and not hers. They are hers, because they belong to her children; they are not hers because the mystery of her innocence is inviolable:

"Not in herself, O daughters; not in herself, I repeat, O daughters; but in us is the Church wounded. Let us then take care that our own lapses do not become wounds for the Church...".

> "Non in se, filiae; non, inquam, in se, filiae, sed in nobis ecclesia vulneratur. Caveamus igitur ne lapsus noster vulnus ecclesiae fiat" (*De virginitate* 48).

The Church always welcomes into her bosom those who are weak and sinful, who are indeed in some regards her privileged children:

"Those who within the Church appear weak, poor, ignorant, sinful even, have a greater need of consideration and must be given more support".

> "Hi qui videntur in ecclesia debiles, pauperes, imprudentes, etiam peccatores, abundantiore indigent honestate et maiore praesidio fulciendi sunt" (*In ps. 118*, 8:54).

Indeed, in a certain sense the Church shoulders responsibility for the sinner and assumes the attitude of the penitent:

"The whole of the Church shoulders the sinner's burden, and must share in his suffering with tears, prayers and pain...".

> "Tota ecclesia suscipit onus peccatoris, cui compatiendum et fletu et oratione et dolore est…" (*De paenitentia* I:81).

"Let it be she who weeps for you; let it be she who pours out tears upon your sins and weeps so greatly that she can find no easy consolation, like those who greatly grieve".

> "Ipsa pro te fleat, ipsa tua peccata deploret et fleat plurimum, ut consolationem non facile admittat, quemadmodum qui plurimum dolent" (*In ps. 37*, 10).

"If you despair of obtaining pardon for grave sins, make use of intercessors, make use of the Church, so that she may pray for you; so that, looking upon her, the Lord may grant that pardon which He might refuse to give to you".

> "Si gravium peccatorum diffidis veniam, adhibe praecatores, adhibe ecclesiam, quae pro te precetur, cuius contemplatione quod tibi dominus negare possit ignoscit" (*In Lucam* V:11).

The Church not only weeps and intercedes, but even actively cures the ills of all, regardless of their social status:

"The Church… not only heals the wounded and tends to those who are weary, but even asperses them with the sweet perfume of grace, pouring out the same grace not only on the rich and powerful, but also upon the plebeian people; she weighs up all with the same balance, welcomes all within her bosom, warms all within the same lap".

> "Ecclesia… non solum saucios curat et lassos fovet, verum etiam suavi gratiae odore respergit, nec divitibus tantum et potioribus sed etiam plebeiae familiae viris eandem transfundit gratiam, aequa omnes lance examinat, omnes eodem sinu suscipit, eodem gremio fovet" (*Ep. extra coll.* 1).

An Appearance of Fallibility

It is undeniable that the Church often appears, to the unenlightened, unfruitful or even corrupt in her work. Sometimes it seems that she achieves little, at others that she is doing deplorable things.

What reply can the believer make in this regard? The following three reflections may be usefully formulated:

First of all, one should recall the law of the lunar nature of the Church, of which we have already spoken:

"The Church has her phases … For she appears to grow weak, like the moon, but it is not so … She may become hidden; she cannot grow weak…".

> "Ecclesia tempora sua habet … Nam videtur sicut luna deficere, sed non deficit … Obumbrari potest, deficere non potest" (*Exameron* IV:7).

Secondly, we should never forget that the fruits of the true activity of the Church belong to the Kingdom of God, which today is invisible, and thus not apparent to the eyes of the world:

"The Church appears to be sterile in this world because she does not generate things which are of the world and the present moment, but which belong to the future; that is to say things which are invisible rather than visible".

> "Ecclesia sterilis videtur in hoc saeculo, quia non saecularia parturit nec praesentia, sed futura; hoc est non ea quae videntur, sed quae non videntur" (*De Abraham* II:72).

Yet the most profound theological reason is that the Church is called, within the plan of the Father, to revive and prolong within her own life the mystery of the *kenosis* of Christ. Even He, if judged according to worldly criteria, did not have much success in His mission; and even He was considered by the worldly powers of His day to be a sinner:

"The Church... rightly assumes the appearance of a sinner, because even Christ Himself assumed the likeness of a sinner".

> "Ecclesia... merito speciem accipit peccatricis, quia Christus quoque formam peccatoris accepit" (*In Lucam* VI:21).

Conclusion

I have put forward this exploration, which has covered practically all of the works of St. Ambrose, as a first attempt at tackling an area which requires urgent attention, in the hope of tempting someone else to pursue this research further.

We have found ourselves faced with an unsystematic treatment; for Ambrose remains a pastor first and foremost. Yet it is undeniable that his reflections are, at the same time, lucid and passionate. Furthermore, it must be said (in contradiction to the pretty well unfounded opinion circulating amongst theologians these days) that it is an *original* reflection: original in its intuitions, its imagery and its emphases; and expressed within works which Erasmus of Rotterdam, who certainly knew what he was talking about, judged to be "aliis inimitabilis".

The "rediscovery" of this holy doctor could well be a remedy for those rather bloodless studies of the Church which are sometimes published nowadays, or for the sort of opinions about the Church which are widespread today; opinions which, rather than being about the Church, are about "ecclesiasticity".

There is little talk in the Christianity of today (the good intentions expressed by the fathers of the Second Vatican Council notwithstanding) of the "mysterious" nature of the Church, i.e. her *truest* nature. She has, perhaps with the intention of preserving herself from apologeticism and triumphalism, ended up by giving an undeserved prevalence to juridicalism and sociologism. There are even those who think that the contemplation of the transcendent *res* of the Church is the indulgence of a sort of Platonism that it is not even worth trying to propose to the contemporary mentality; it remains instead the exclusive property of *sacra doctrina*[13].

Jesus, Head of the renewed Humanity which is incorporated in Him, and which finds in Him the ever active principle of Redemption and universal unification, does not live in an improbable *Hyperouranios*: He sits at the right hand of the Father and is forever in the act of pouring out the Spirit which gives the Church its identity and concreteness. Nor is the "Christus totus", born from this perennial Pentecost, an outmoded metaphysical hypothesis: it is the sole reality that truly merits our attention as explorers of God's plan.

I must state once again at this stage what I have already pointed out several times elsewhere; that the concept of the "People of God" – a concept which is furthermore fundamental and unrenouncible – is insufficient to give us an adequate understanding of the nature of the

---

[13] The most radical formulation of this odd "non-theological theology" is offered by Küng: "The true essence of the church is realised in non-being" (*op. cit.*, p. 31). Having denied any transcendent reality to the Church, it is understandable that his discourse becomes purely phenomenological.

Church. Von Balthasar has already noted that, if we only make use of the idea of the "People of God" when explaining the Church, then we can no longer distinguish her from the Synagogue (Introduction to *Sponsa Verbi*).

In fact many people, depicting the Church as just the "servant" and the "guardian" of the Divine Word, reduce her to being the annunciation and the prophecy of the Kingdom, presenting her insistently as an organism conditioned by history, and for this reason capable of faults and open to criticism; it does not occur to them to elaborate anything other than "synagogology". As if the Lord Jesus had not already consummated His sacrifice of renewal, and as if the indissoluble marriage between the firstborn Son of the Father and redeemed Humanity had not already been celebrated[14].

St. Ambrose is not the easiest of writers, and he often remains impervious to our reading of him; but returning to his company may well help us all to get back on the right track.

In particular, this might encourage theologians – and especially ecclesiologists – to dedicate themselves to that

---

[14] The sin at the origin of this "non-theological" perspective is holding that the Truth of the Church can be drawn *not* from her intrinsic relationship with Christ (as is taught by Revelation), but from her – necessary, but certainly not constitutive – relationship with the World; not from her relationship of quasi-immanence with the "Kingdom" ("Ecclesia seu Regnum Dei iam praesens in mysterio", as it says in *Lumen Gentium* 3), but from her undeniable involvement in "History". In this way, while they believe that they are taking a snapshot of the King's Bride, they end up just getting a shot of her wardrobe: the shabby and dusty garments in which our wretchedness so fatally dresses her.

most relevant and useful of their tasks, which is that of exciting, nourishing and justifying within our minds astonishment, joy and enthusiasm for God's plan, and for the destiny which has been assigned to us through it.